ANGRY earth

DESTRUCTIVE HURRICANES

By Michael Portman

Gareth Stevens
Publishing

Please visit our website, www.garethstevens.com. For a free color catalog of all our high-quality books, call toll free 1-800-542-2595 or fax 1-877-542-2596.

Library of Congress Cataloging-in-Publication Data

Portman, Michael, 1976-
Destructive hurricanes / Michael Portman.
    p. cm. — (Angry Earth)
Includes index.
ISBN 978-1-4339-6539-5 (pbk.)
ISBN 978-1-4339-6540-1 (6-pack)
ISBN 978-1-4339-6537-1 (library binding)
1. Hurricanes—Juvenile literature. I. Title.
QC944.2.P67 2012
551.55'2—dc23
                                        2011028781

First Edition

Published in 2012 by
Gareth Stevens Publishing
111 East 14th Street, Suite 349
New York, NY 10003

Copyright © 2012 Gareth Stevens Publishing

Designer: Katelyn E. Reynolds
Editor: Therese Shea

Photo credits: Cover, pp. 1, 4, 5 (main), 6, 7, 12 (inset), 23 (inset), (cover, pp. 1, 3–32 background and newspaper graphics) Shutterstock.com; p. 5 (inset) Buyenlarge/Getty Images; pp. 8, 16 Dorling Kindersley/Getty Images; p. 9 Sergio Dionisio/Getty Images; p. 11 (inset) Brandon Laufenberg/iStock Vectors/Getty Images; p. 11 (main) Mike Theiss/National Geographic/Getty Images; p. 12 (main) Adalberto Roque/AFP/Getty Images; pp. 13, 19 (inset) Joe Raedle/Getty Images; p. 15 (inset) Erik S. Lesser/Getty Images; pp. 15 (main), 17, 28 NOAA via Getty Images; p. 19 (main) DAJ/Getty Images; p. 20 Mark Wilson/Getty Images; p. 21 Stephen Morton/Getty Images; pp. 22–23 Stephen Alvarez/National Geographic/Getty Images; p. 24 Monika Graff/Getty Images; p. 25 (inset) John Loengard/Time & Life Pictures/Getty Images; p. 25 (main) Richard Kaylin/Stone/Getty Images; p. 26 Linda Rosier/NY Daily News Archive via Getty Images; p. 27 David J. Phillips/AFP/Getty Images; p. 29 (inset), (cover, pp. 1, 3–32 text/image box graphic) iStockphoto.com; p. 29 (main) POOL/AFP/Getty Images.

Printed in the United States of America

CPSIA compliance information: Batch #CW12GS: For further information contact Gareth Stevens, New York, New York at 1-800-542-2595.

CONTENTS

Words in the glossary appear in **bold** type the first time they are used in the text.

A FORCE OF NATURE

Hurricanes are one of the most powerful and **destructive** forces in nature. Every year, hurricanes cause billions of dollars of property **damage**. They destroy buildings, bridges, and vehicles. Hurricane winds knock down trees and rip apart power lines. Hurricane rains cause floods that wash away roads, coastlines, and even hills. Some hurricanes are powerful enough to destroy whole cities. Not surprisingly, people face great dangers from hurricanes, too.

In order to understand how these destructive storms form, it's important to first understand the water cycle. It's also key to learn how **air pressure** and weather systems work together to create hurricanes.

Hurricane Ike, Florida (2008)

Deadliest US Hurricane

On September 8, 1900, a powerful hurricane struck Galveston, Texas. The entire city was flooded, and most of it was destroyed. It's thought that more than 6,000 people were killed. To this day, this hurricane is the deadliest natural **disaster** in US history.

People who live on or near beaches are encouraged to evacuate, or leave, to escape the dangers of a hurricane.

THE WATER CYCLE

The water cycle begins when the sun's rays warm water on Earth's surface, turning some of it into water vapor. This process is called evaporation. As water vapor rises into the cool upper atmosphere, it turns back into liquid or frozen water. This process, called condensation, is how clouds form. When water drops or ice crystals inside clouds get too heavy, they fall back to Earth as rain, hail, sleet, or snow. This is called precipitation. Then the cycle begins again.

Hurricanes and the rainstorms they bring are part of the water cycle. They move huge amounts of water from one place to another.

Transpiration

Water doesn't have to be on Earth's surface to evaporate. It can also evaporate from plants, especially plant leaves. This process is called transpiration, and it's another part of the water cycle. Studies show that about 10 percent of the water vapor in the atmosphere is from transpiration.

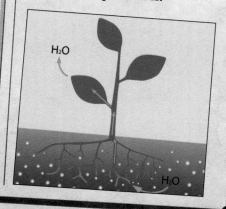

▲
The amount of water on Earth has remained
the same for hundreds of millions of years.

7

AIR PRESSURE

The air we breathe is made up of tiny, invisible **particles**. Even though we don't feel them, air particles have weight, just like everything else on Earth. The weight of air particles as they press down on Earth creates air pressure.

Air pressure depends on how many air particles occupy a space. This amount changes as air temperature changes. Cool air sinks and contracts, drawing air particles closer together. This creates high pressure. Warm air rises and spreads out, causing air particles to move farther apart. This creates low pressure.

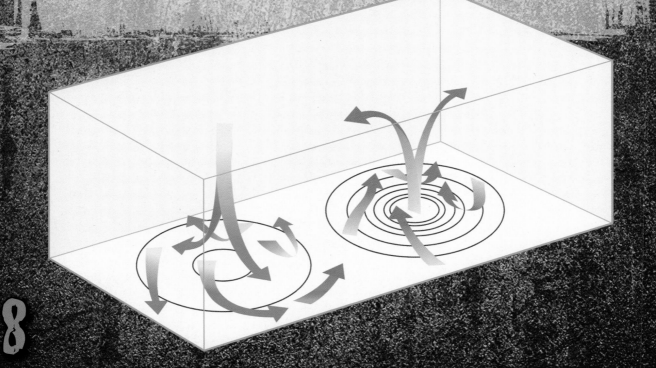

Humidity

Humidity is the amount of water vapor in the air. Water vapor can change air pressure, though it has a smaller effect than temperature. Air with more water vapor is lighter than air with less water vapor. As humidity increases, air pressure decreases. As humidity decreases, air pressure increases.

Fog may occur when the humidity in the air is very high.

9

One way to **predict** weather is to measure air pressure. Usually, high-pressure systems mean that weather will be calm and skies will be clear. Low-pressure systems often bring warmer, stormy weather. Hurricanes usually begin their life as small storms caused by low-pressure systems.

Hurricanes form over ocean waters that are at least 80°F (27°C). As warm, moist air rises, cooler air sinks to take its place. Once that air becomes warm, it also rises. More cool wind rushes in, and wind speed increases as the air cycles. The moist air creates clouds and thunderstorms called **tropical disturbances.**

Different Names

Hurricanes, tropical cyclones, and typhoons are all the same thing! "Hurricane" is the term used for severe storms over the Atlantic Ocean. In some parts of the Pacific Ocean, hurricanes are called typhoons. In other parts of the Pacific Ocean and in the Indian Ocean, hurricanes are called tropical cyclones.

These dark clouds are the outer edge of a hurricane forming over the Caribbean Sea.

weather map showing high-pressure system (H) and low-pressure system (L)

Spinning Winds

Once a hurricane forms, it's largely steered by the global winds that blow across the oceans. These allow forecasters to predict a hurricane's path. Hurricanes spin counterclockwise above the equator. Below the equator, they spin clockwise.

Countries surrounded by warm waters are often threatened by hurricanes. These people walk through the rains of Hurricane Lili, which hit Cuba in 2002.

A tropical disturbance can only grow stronger if it remains above warm water. A tropical disturbance with a wind speed of 23 miles (37 km) per hour is called a **tropical depression**. If wind speed reaches 39 miles (63 km) per hour, the tropical depression becomes a **tropical storm**.

Once winds reach 74 miles (119 km) per hour, the storm is labeled a hurricane. Sometimes this happens very quickly, in just a few hours. Other times, it can take several days for a hurricane to form. As long as the winds keep spinning, a hurricane is a possibility.

tropical storm over Miami, Florida (2010)

HURRICANE SEASON

Each year, between 40 and 50 ocean storms turn into hurricanes. Because hurricanes require warm water and warm air, they usually only form during a certain time of the year. This period is called hurricane season. The official hurricane season lasts from June 1 to November 30. However, hurricanes can occur before or after those dates. In the Atlantic Ocean, the majority of hurricanes occur from August to October.

Fortunately, most hurricanes never make it to land. Sometimes the wind blows them back out to sea. Other times, a hurricane may hit an area of cold water that causes it to weaken.

Hurricane Alley

Most hurricanes in the Atlantic Ocean form over a band of warm water that stretches from Africa to Central America. This area is sometimes called Hurricane Alley. Scientists have noticed that the water in Hurricane Alley has been getting warmer. They worry that this may cause even more hurricanes to form.

a scientist tracking hurricanes

This image from the National Oceanic and Atmospheric Administration (NOAA) highlights warm ocean waters in red. Several hurricanes and tropical storms can be seen in this band.

HURRICANE PARTS

The center of a hurricane is called the eye. The eye of a hurricane is usually about 20 to 30 miles (32 to 48 km) wide. Perhaps surprisingly, the low-pressure air in the eye means that it's very calm.

Surrounding the eye is a ring of clouds and thunderstorms called the eye wall. The eye wall is where the strongest winds are found.

Rain bands make up the rest of the hurricane. They spiral out from the eye wall. They can range from a few miles to tens of miles wide and from 50 to 300 miles (80 to 483 km) long. Rain bands bring heavy rain, wind, and even tornadoes.

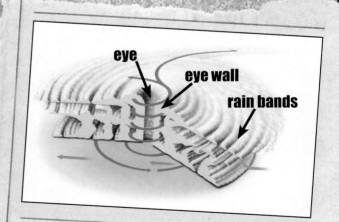

eye

eye wall

rain bands

The image below shows Hurricane Rita over the Gulf of Mexico in 2005. You can clearly see the eye in the center of the system.

▼

A Big Eye

The tallest part of a hurricane is the eye wall. Some eye walls can reach 50,000 feet (15,240 m) into the air! How tall is that? The tallest mountain in the world, Mount Everest, is 29,035 feet (8,850 m) tall. This means a hurricane may tower above Mount Everest!

HURRICANE NAMES AND CATEGORIES

It's common for several hurricanes or tropical storms to occur in different parts of the ocean at the same time. To avoid confusion, every tropical storm is given a name. If a tropical storm becomes a hurricane, it keeps its name. Over the years, names were chosen in many different ways. Today, forecasters take names in order from a list.

Forecasters also use a scale to show how powerful a hurricane is. This scale is called the Saffir-Simpson Scale, and it's divided into five **categories**. A Category 1 hurricane is the least destructive, while a Category 5 is the most destructive.

Name That Hurricane

Hurricane names are chosen from several different lists. Different parts of the world use different lists. For instance, the Atlantic Ocean list is different from the one used for the Pacific. In the Atlantic, the names are listed alphabetically and switch between male and female. There are no names that begin with the letters Q, U, X, Y, or Z.

National Hurricane Center in Miami, Florida

SAFFIR-SIMPSON SCALE

CATEGORY	WIND SPEED	DAMAGE
1	74–95 MPH	Some Damage
2	96–110 MPH	Moderate Damage
3	111–130 MPH	Extensive Damage
4	131–155 MPH	Extreme Damage
5	155+ MPH	Catastrophic Damage

▲ The catastrophic damage of a Category 5 hurricane can cause widespread destruction. People are instructed to evacuate areas on low ground within many miles of the shoreline.

WHY ARE HURRICANES DANGEROUS?

Once they hit land, hurricanes cause damage in many ways. Powerful winds can snap trees and power lines, cutting off roads and electricity. Buildings that aren't constructed to withstand heavy winds are often no match for a hurricane. A hurricane can turn ordinary objects such as signs, branches, and pieces of wood into dangerous flying objects. Sometimes, hurricanes can even cause tornadoes to form.

As a hurricane reaches shore, its winds can push a large wall of water onto land. This is called a storm surge. Storm surges can cause severe flooding. In addition to wind, hurricanes bring huge amounts of rain that can also cause flooding.

Away from Water

Hurricanes begin to weaken and die once they hit land. However, strong winds and heavy rainfall can still cause damage for hundreds of miles as the storm moves across land. A hurricane can also regain strength if it moves back over water after hitting land.

A hurricane can dump over a foot (30 cm) of rain in a day. This road near a canal in New Orleans, Louisiana, flooded after Hurricane Gustav struck in 2008.

RAILROAD CROSSING

SPEED LIMIT

HURRICANE PLANES

Since the 1960s, **satellites** have been used to track hurricanes. But satellites don't always tell forecasters enough to categorize a hurricane. To get more exact information, US Air Force Reserve pilots fly special planes directly into hurricanes. These planes collect **data**, such as wind speed and air pressure. A plane may make several trips through a hurricane.

NOAA uses special jets to fly around and above hurricanes. The planes' instruments help forecasters predict a hurricane's path by measuring the winds that guide the hurricane.

These hurricane planes are ready for action at Keesler Air Force Base in Mississippi.

Flying into Danger

The US military began flying planes through hurricanes in 1944. That year, planes from the navy and the army tracked a hurricane as it moved from Puerto Rico to the northeastern United States. The information that resulted allowed people to prepare for the hurricane and saved many lives.

HISTORIC HURRICANES

The United States has been hit by many powerful hurricanes over the years. One of the most damaging was Hurricane Camille. In August 1969, this hurricane struck the coast of Mississippi as a Category 5 event. Its winds were so strong they destroyed all the instruments used to measure wind speed. However, based on other information, experts think the wind speeds reached 200 miles (322 km) per hour.

In August 1992, Hurricane Andrew ripped across south Florida. The Category 4 winds destroyed much in the hurricane's path, including wind-speed instruments. After passing over Florida, Andrew continued across the Gulf of Mexico until it hit the Louisiana coast.

Irene's Impact

In August 2011, Hurricane Irene created a wide path of destruction from North Carolina to Vermont. Irene's rains caused major flooding. Roads and bridges were carried away by water. Hundreds of thousands of people had to evacuate their homes.

home destroyed by Hurricane Camille

Hurricane Andrew destroyed about 126,000 houses and left about 180,000 people homeless. It caused more than $26.5 billion in damage in Florida and Louisiana alone.

25

HURRICANE KATRINA

When Hurricane Katrina hit Florida on August 25, 2005, it wasn't a very powerful hurricane. However, once it passed through Florida and entered the Gulf of Mexico, it began to strengthen. On August 28, Katrina turned into a Category 5 hurricane. By the time it hit Louisiana on August 29, it had dropped to Category 3 but was still packing a powerful punch. Katrina then continued its destructive path through Louisiana and into Mississippi before it weakened and died.

Florida, Louisiana, Mississippi, and Alabama all suffered severe wind damage from Hurricane Katrina. Storm surges caused flooding along the coasts of Mississippi and Louisiana.

New Orleans neighborhood after Hurricane Katrina

Still Suffering

Hurricane Katrina was the most expensive storm in US history. It caused over $75 billion in damage. Most of the city of New Orleans, Louisiana, was flooded, with 20 feet (6 m) of water covering some areas. New Orleans and many other places are still recovering from the damage today.

◁ This photo was taken about 2 weeks after Hurricane Katrina hit. The streets of New Orleans were hard hit by floods.

HURRICANE SAFETY

If you live in an area where hurricanes are known to strike, it's important to be prepared. Be sure to keep emergency supplies of food, water, and rain gear in your home. Since hurricanes often cause power loss, it's also a good idea to have a flashlight, a battery-powered radio, and a first-aid kit.

Always listen to authorities before, during, and after a hurricane. If you're told to leave an area, be sure to do so quickly. Return to your home only after you've been told it's safe. The more you know about hurricanes, the better prepared you will be if one occurs near you.

Where They Strike

In the United States, hurricanes can hit anywhere along the Atlantic coast and the coast of the Gulf of Mexico. No hurricane has ever hit the Pacific coast of the United States. However, tropical storms and hurricanes have struck the Pacific coast of Mexico. Sometimes, rain from those storms reaches into California.

A Coast Guard helicopter carries a New Orleans resident to safety following Hurricane Katrina.

emergency supplies

GLOSSARY

air pressure: downward pressure applied by the weight of air

category: a division within a system for grouping or organizing

damage: harm. Also, to cause harm.

data: information in the form of facts or figures

destructive: causing damage

disaster: an event that causes serious loss or destruction

particle: a very small bit of something

predict: to guess what will happen in the future based on facts or knowledge

satellite: an object that circles Earth in order to send and receive data

tropical depression: a low-pressure system over warm ocean waters with winds of 23 to 38 miles (37 to 61 km) per hour

tropical disturbance: a weather event over warm ocean waters that lasts at least 24 hours and doesn't have continuous winds

tropical storm: a low-pressure system over warm ocean waters with winds between 39 and 73 miles (63 and 117 km) per hour

FOR MORE INFORMATION

Books

Hirschmann, Kris. *Hurricane!* Edina, MN: ABDO Publishing, 2008.

Hoffman, Mary Ann. *Hurricane Katrina*. New York, NY: PowerKids Press, 2007.

Simon, Seymour. *Hurricanes*. New York, NY: Collins, 2007.

Websites

How Hurricanes Work
science.howstuffworks.com/nature/natural-disasters/hurricane.htm
Read many interesting facts about hurricanes and the science behind them.

Hurricanes
www.weatherwizkids.com/weather-hurricane.htm
Learn about hurricane science, hurricanes past and present, hurricane hunters, and much more.

Tropical Twisters
kids.earth.nasa.gov/archive/hurricane/
Learn how hurricanes are created, how they move, and how dangerous they are.

INDEX